STUDENT BUDGET Guide

Step-By-Step Strategies To Mastering Financial Independence For Scholars

By

JOHN O. SILAS

Copyright © 2024 by John O. Silas

All rights reserved. No part of this book may be reproduced, distributed, or transmitted in any form or by any means, including photocopying, recording, or other electronic or mechanical methods, without the prior written permission of the publisher, except in the case of brief quotations embodied in critical reviews and certain other noncommercial uses permitted by copyright law.

The information in this book is true and complete to the best of our knowledge. All recommendations are made without guarantee on the part of the author or publisher. The author and publisher disclaim any liability in connection with the use of this information.

Dedicated to my daughter C.R.O; and to my mentor who taught me the value of saving and budgeting. His wisdom and guidance have inspired me to help others achieve financial stability.

May the knowledge and strategies shared in these pages empower you to take control of your financial journey. May you achieve financial stability, independence, and success. May you use this book as a tool to build a brighter financial future, and create a life of purpose and fulfillment for yourself.

Sincerely
John O. Silas

TABLE OF CONTENTS

Part 1:
Understanding Budgeting Basics

1 Definition And Purpose 1
   Purpose of budgeting

2 Importance of Budgeting For Students 3
   Types of budgets
   Benefits of budgets

3 Financial Literacy for students 7
   Basic financial Concepts
   Common financial mistakes
   Building a healthy financial mindset

4 Analyzing Income 9
   Sources of income
   Calculating and forming monthly income

(continued on next page)

| 5 | **Tracking Your Expenses** | 11 |

    Fixed vs variable expenses
    Essential vs non-essential spending
    Tools for tracking expenses

| 6 | **Understand Debts** | 13 |

Types of debts
Impact of debts on your finances
Strategies for managing and reducing debts

Part 2:
Creating Your Budget

| 7 | **Setting Financial Goals** | 17 |

    Short term Vs long-term financial goals
    S-M-A-R-T goals framework
    Prioritize your goals

| 8 | **Building Your Budget** | 19 |

The 50/30/20 rule
Zero based
Creating a personalized budget template

(continued)

9	**Adjusting Your Budget And Emergency Fund**	21

Adapting to Changes in income and expenses
Seasonal and one time expenses
Emergency fund planning
Why do you need an emergency fund
How much should you save
Where to keep your emergency fund
Tips for building your emergency fund
Common mistakes to avoid

Part 3: Practical Tips And Strategies

10	**Saving Money On A Student Budget**	25

Finding student discounts
Saving on textbook and supplies
Affordable meal planning
Benefits of meal planning
Tips for Affordable meal planning
Budget-friendly meal ideas
Grocery shopping on a budget

(continued)

11   Frugal Living Tips   29

Cost effective housing options
Entertainment on a budget
Second hand shopping
Benefits of second-hand shopping
Tips for second hand shopping
Secondhand shopping essentials for students

12   Increasing Your Income   33

    Part-time jobs and gigs
    Freelancing opportunities
    Scholarships and grants
    What are scholarships
    Types of scholarships
    What are grants
    Types of grants
    Tips for Applying
    Additional resources

(continued)

13	**Investment Basics For Students**	37

    Introduction to Investing
    Why Invest
    Investment options
    Investing strategies
    Getting started
    Risk Management
    Micro investing apps and resources

14	**Planning For The Future**	41

    Building credits
    Understanding Insurance
    Saving for major life events
    Create a long term savings plan
    Strategies for long term savings
    Additional tips

Part 4:
Utilizing Resources And Tools

15	**Building Tools And Apps**	45

    Choosing the right tool for you

(continued)

Part 5: Staying Motivated And Overcoming Challenges

16 Staying On Track — 53
Building good financial habits
Accountability partners and groups
Rewarding yourself Smartly
Ideas for rewards

17 Overcoming Common Challenges — 59
Dealing with peer pressure
Coping with financial Stress
Strategies for staying motivated
More tips for self-motivation

Part 6: Reflection

18 Reflecting On Your Financial Journey — 65
Celebrating your achievements
Continuing your financial education

Glossary

FORWARD

Welcome to the ultimate guide to taking control of your finances as a student! As you navigate the challenges of higher education, managing your money can seem like an overwhelming task. But with the right tools, you can achieve financial stability, reduce stress, and focus on what matters most - your education and future.

Whether you are a freshman or a graduate student this book is designed to be your trusted companion that will help you make informed decisions on your journey to financial independence. Inside, you will find practical advice, expert tips, and strategies on budgeting, saving, investing, and much more.
(continued on next page)

The author has done an excellent job of breaking down complex financial concepts into straight forward easy-to-understand language with bulletpoints, making this book accessible to students from all backgrounds. The advice is actionable, the examples are relatable, and the tone is supportive and encouraging.

By reading this book, you'll gain the confidence and knowledge to take charge of your finances, achieve your goals, and build a brighter future. Shall we begin on this financial journey together?

INTRODUCTION

Managing your finances as a student can be daunting, especially with the myriad of expenses and limited income sources. Yet, mastering the art of budgeting is crucial for financial stability and success, both during your college years and beyond. This book, "Student Budget Guide," is designed to guide you through the essentials of personal finance with practical, easy-to-follow advice tailored specifically for students.

In these pages, you'll discover how to set achievable financial goals, track your income and expenses, and make informed spending decisions. You'll learn effective strategies for saving money, managing debt, and even boosting your income through side gigs and scholarships. Whether you're new to budgeting or looking to refine your financial habits, this book offers the tools and insights you need to take control of your money.

Empower yourself with the knowledge and confidence to manage your finances wisely. Let's embark on this journey and build a strong foundation for your financial future.

PART 1: UNDERSTANDING BUDGETING BASICS

Chapter 1: Definition And Purpose

Budgeting is the process of creating a plan to spend your money. This spending plan called a budget, helps you determine in advance whether you will have enough money to do the things you need to do or would like to do.

Budgeting is critical for successful financial management. The **Purpose Of Budgeting** is to provide a clear picture of your financial situation and outcome in the following ways:

- Budgetting for both short and long-term expenses.
- Making sure you are living within what you can afford.
- Saving for future goals and emergencies

And it also helps you:
1. Manage Finances Effectively: Track income and expenses to understand where each of the money is going.
2. Prioritize Needs Over Wants: Allocate resources to essential expenses (tuition, room, board) before discretionary spending (entertainment, hobbies).
3. Achieve Financial Goals: Save for short-term goals (textbooks, spring break) and long-term goals (graduation, career).
4. Develop Financial Literacy: Learn essential skills for lifelong financial management and responsibility.
5. Make Smart Financial Decisions: Balance academic and personal responsibilities with financial obligations.
6. Build Credit And Savings: Establish a strong financial foundation for post-graduation life.

Budgeting allows you to get control of your finances, make the most use of your resources, and position yourself for financial success during and after college.

Chapter 2:
Importance of Budgeting for Students

Budgeting is often seen as a daunting task, but it's a vital skill that can set the foundation for a stable financial future. As a student, you may face unique financial challenges, limited income, student loan debts, and fluctuating expenses. Learning to budget can help you navigate these challenges and also help in:

- Preventing Debt Accumulation: By keeping track of your spending and staying within your means, you can avoid unnecessary debt and interest payments.

- Reducing Stress: Financial instability may serve as a major source of stress. A well-planned budget gives you a clear picture of your finances, reducing anxiety and helping you make informed decisions.

- Priotizing Expenses And Achieving Financial Goals: Whether saving for a textbook, a trip, a new laptop, or your first apartment after graduation, a budget helps you allocate resources toward your goals.

- Building Good Habits: The financial habits you develop now will carry on into your future. Budgeting teaches discipline, planning, and prioritization, which are essential skills in all areas of life.
- Manage Limited Financial Resources: Make the most of limited income, scholarships, and loans.
- Increase Financial Flexibility: Create a safety net for unexpected expenses or opportunities.
- Enhance Academic Performance: Reduce financial distractions and focus on studies.

Types Of Budgets

There are various types of budgets, each serving different purposes, namely:

1. Personal Budget: A plan for an individual's or household's income and expenses.
2. Operating Budget: Used by businesses to plan for day-to-day expenses.
3. Capital Budget: Focuses on long-term investments and expenditures, such as purchasing equipment or investing in infrastructure.

For students, a personal budget is most relevant. It includes tracking your income (such as part-time job earnings, allowances, or student loans) and your expenses (such as tuition, rent, groceries, and entertainment).

Benefits Of Budgets

Budgeting offers numerous benefits which include:

- Financial Awareness: Helps you understand where your money is going and identify areas where you can cut costs.
- Goal Achievement: Assists in setting and achieving financial goals, such as saving for a vacation or paying off a student loan.
- Stress Reduction: Reduces financial anxiety by providing a clear plan for managing money.
- Improved Spending Habits: Encourages mindful spending and helps avoid impulsive purchases.
- Financial Confidence: Develop a healthy relationship with money and feel empowered to achieve financial goals.
- Improved Credit Score: Establish a positive credit history.

- Financial Stability: Manage finances effectively and avoid debt.
- Increased Savings: Build an emergency fund and save for goals.
- Improved Financial Literacy: Develop essential skills for lifelong financial management.
- Better Time Management: Prioritize expenses and allocate time effectively.

- Enhanced Academic Performance: Reduce financial distractions and focus on studies.
- Increased Financial Flexibility: Create a safety net for unexpected expenses or opportunities.
- Avoidance Of Debt Traps: Minimize reliance on high-interest loans and credit cards.
- Long-term Financial Security: Establish a strong financial foundation for post-graduation life.
- Independence: Take control of finances and make independent decisions.

- Peace Of Mind: Feel confident and secure in financial decisions.
- Ability To Afford Extras: Enjoy discretionary spending, like entertainment or travel.

Chapter 3:
Financial Literacy For Students

Basic Financial Concepts

Understanding basic financial concepts is crucial for effective budgeting. Here are some key terms that you need to be aware of:

- Income: Money obtained regularly, usually from labor or investments.

- Expenses: Money spent on goods and services.

- Savings: The portion of income not spent on current expenditures.

- Debt: Money owed to another person or institution.

- Credit: The ability to borrow money or access goods or services with the understanding that you will pay later.

Common Financial Mistakes

Students often make several common financial mistakes some of which are:

- Overspending on Non-essentials: Spending too much on eating out, entertainment, or shopping.
- Ignoring Small Expenses: Small, frequent purchases can add up quickly.
- Using Credit Unwisely: Accumulating high-interest debt through credit cards or loans without a clear plan to pay them off.
- Failing to Save: Not setting aside money for emergencies or future needs.

Building A Healthy Financial Mindset

Developing a healthy financial mindset involves:

- Being Disciplined: Sticking to your budget and resisting the temptation to overspend.
- Prioritizing Needs Over Wants: Differentiating between essential and non-essential expenses.
- Staying Informed: Educating yourself about personal finance and staying up-to-date with financial news.
- Setting Realistic Goals: Establishing achievable financial goals and working towards them consistently.

Chapter 4:
Analyzing Income

Sources Of Income

As a student, your income might come from various sources which may include:

- Allowances: Regular financial support from family.
- Part-time Jobs: Earnings from working while studying.
- Scholarships and Grants: Financial awards given for academic or other achievements.
- Student Loans: Borrowed money that must be repaid.

Calculating And Forming A Monthly Income

To create an effective budget, you need to calculate your total monthly income. This involves:

- Listing all sources of income. eg, scholarships, grants, part-time job wages, allowance from parents or guardians, internship stipends, and any other regular income.

- Estimating the amount received from each source.
- Determining the frequency of each income source: weekly, biweekly, monthly, semester-based (e.g., scholarships).
- Analyzing and summing these amounts to get your total monthly income. Eg,
  -Weekly income: multiply by 4= 1 month income.
  -Biweekly income: multiply by 2= 1 month income.
  -Semester-based income: divided by the number of months in the semester (e.g., 4-5 months and there you will get the idea of your monthly income.

To be more elaborate:
-Part-time job: $1,000 biweekly (multiply by 2) = $2,000/month
-Scholarship: $4,000/semester (divide by 4) = $1,000/month
- Allowance: $500/month
-Total monthly income = $2,000 + $1,000 + $500 = $3,500.

Remember to adjust your calculation if your income sources change during the year (e.g., summer job, internship.

Chapter 5:
Tracking Your Expenses

Fixed Vs Variable Expenses

Expenses could be classified as fixed and variable.
- Fixed Expenses: Regular, unchanging costs such as rent, tuition, insurance, etcetera.

- Variable Expenses: Fluctuating costs such as groceries, utilities, entertainment, etc.

And it's important to distinguish between:
Essential Vs Non-essential Spending
- Essential Spending: Necessary expenses for living and studying, like housing, food, textbooks, study fees and materials, food and groceries, phone and Internet, health, laundry, transportation, self-care, etc.

- Non-essential Spending: Discretionary expenses such as dining out, hobbies, vacations, social events, impulse buying, unnecessary subscriptions, overspending on clothes, gadgets, accessories, and the list goes on.

Tools For Tracking Expenses

Some various ways and tools can help you track your expenses, such as:

- Spreadsheets: Software programs that allow users to store, organize, and analyze data in a table format. Eg, Microsoft Excel, Google Sheets, Apple Numbers.
- Budgeting Apps: Applications like Mint, YNAB (You Need a Budget), PocketGuard, etc.
- Bank Statements: frequent review of your bank and credit card statements to monitor spending.
- Planners And Calenders: Use them to track expenses and stay organized.
- Photos: Take pictures of receipts with your phone to keep a record.
- Reminders: To review and update your budget regularly.
- Notepads: Get a small notebook to record daily expenses.
- Envelopes and Jars: Set up a budgeting system using envelopes or jars for different categories (e.g., food, entertainment).
- Digital Wallets: Apple Wallet, Google Pay, Samsung Pay.
- Online Budgeting Tools: Apps from banks, NerdWallet's Budget Calculator. etc.

Chapter 6: Understanding Debt

Debt is a common financial tool, but understanding how it works is crucial, especially for students managing limited budgets.

Types Of Debts

Students often encounter different types of debt such as:

- Student Loans: Borrowed money specifically for education, usually with lower interest rates and flexible repayment terms.
- Credit Cards: Convenient but can lead to high-interest debt if not managed properly.
- Personal Loans: Non-specific loans that can be used for various expenses, often with higher interest rates.

Impact Of Debts On Your Finances

Debt can have negative significant effects on your financial situation leading to:

- Increased Expenses: Debt repayments reduce the amount of disposable income.
- Financial Stress: Debt can cause anxiety and stress, affecting mental health and academic performance.
- Limited Financial Flexibility: Debt can reduce your ability to make choices about spending, saving, or investing.
- Poor Credit Score: Missed payments or high credit utilization can harm your credit score, affecting future loan or credit opportunities.
- Accumulating Interest: Unpaid debts can lead to interest accumulation, increasing the total amount owed.
- Reduced Savings: Debt payments can leave little room for saving or building an emergency fund.
- Delayed Financial Goals: Debt can postpone achieving financial goals, such as buying a car, traveling, or graduating debt-free.
- Increased Debt Cycle: Missed payments or accumulating interest can lead to a cycle of debt, making it harder to escape

- Impact On Academic Performance: Financial stress can distract from studies, leading to poor academic performance.
- Long-term Financial Consequences: Unmanaged debt can affect your financial stability and creditworthiness after graduation.

Strategies For Managing And Reducing Debts
To manage and reduce debt effectively:

- Create a Repayment Plan: Pay off high-interest debt first.
- Consolidate Debt: Combine multiple debts into one with a lower interest rate.
- Avoid New Debt: Limit the use of credit cards and avoid unnecessary loans.
- Seek Advice: Consult financial advisors or use campus financial resources for guidance.
- Borrow only what's necessary.
- Understand loan terms and interest rates.
- Create a budget and debt repayment plan.

- Prioritize needs over wants.
- Seek financial assistance or counseling.
- Explore debt consolidation or forgiveness options.

Remember, managing debt effectively is crucial to maintaining financial stability and achieving long-term financial goals.

Understanding these budgeting essentials will allow you to take control of your finances and set yourself up for financial success throughout your student years and beyond.

PART 2: CREATING YOUR BUDGET

Chapter 7: Setting Financial Goals

Short-term Vs Long-term Financial Goals

Setting financial goals is a vital step in budget creation. These goals can be categorized as:

*Short-term Goals: These are goals you aim to achieve within a year. Examples include saving for a new laptop, a summer vacation, or paying off a credit card debt.

*Long-term Goals: These goals span over a longer period, typically more than a year. Examples include saving for a car, planning for graduate school, or creating an emergency fund.

S-M-A-R-T Goals Framework

To ensure your financial goals are clear and achievable, use the SMART framework:

> **Specific:** Define the goal clearly. Instead of just mentioning "save money," say "save $300 for a new computer."
>
> **Measurable:** Be certain you can monitor your advancement. For instance, "save $50 a month" provides a clear metric.
>
> **Achievable:** Set realistic goals considering your income and expenses.
>
> **Relevant:** Your goals should align with your needs and long-term plans.
>
> **Time-bound:** Set a deadline for achieving your goal, for instance, "save $500 in 10 months."

Prioritize Your Goals

Once you've identified your goals, prioritize them based on urgency and importance. Essential needs and high-interest debt repayments should take precedence over non-essential wants.

Chapter 8:
Building Your Budget

The 50/30/20 Rule

A popular budgeting method is the 50/30/20 rule, which allocates your after-tax income into three categories:

- 50% Needs: Essential expenses like rent, utilities, groceries, and transportation.
- 30% Wants: Discretionary spending such as dining out, hobbies, and entertainment.
- 20% Savings and Debt Repayment: Savings, emergency fund contributions, and debt repayments.

Zero-based

Applying Zero-based budgeting ensures that every dollar of your income is assigned a purpose, leaving you with zero remaining funds at the end of the month. This method involves.

- Listing all income sources.
- Allocating every dollar to expenses, savings, and debt repayment.
- Adjusting until the total income equals the total outflow.

Creating A Personalized Budget Template

To build a personalized budget:

> 1. List Income: Identify all sources of income.
> 2. List Expenses: Categorize your expenses into fixed and variable, essential and non-essential.
> 3. Allocate Funds: Assign amounts to each category based on your goals and priorities.
> 4. Review and Adjust: Review your budget regularly and make any necessary adjustments to keep on target.

Chapter 9: Adjusting Your Budget And Emergency Fund

Adapting To Changes In Income Or Expenses

Life as a student can be unpredictable. You might receive unexpected financial aid or face an unplanned expense. To adapt:

- Flexible Allocation: Have a portion of your budget that can be adjusted as needed.
- Reevaluate Regularly: Review your budget monthly and adjust for any changes in income or expenses.

Seasonal And One Time Expenses

Certain expenses occur infrequently, such as holiday gifts or textbooks at the start of a semester. Plan for these by:

- Setting Aside Funds: Allocate a small amount each month for these irregular expenses.
- Creating a Separate Fund: Maintain a separate savings account for one-time expenses.

Emergency Fund Planning

As a student, unexpected expenses can arise at any time, threatening to disrupt your financial stability. That's where an emergency fund comes in – a safety net to help you navigate unexpected expenses and stay on track with your budget.

Why Do You Need An Emergency Fund

1. For Unexpected Expenses: Car repairs, medical bills, or apartment damages can occur suddenly, and an emergency fund helps you cover these costs.
2. For Financial Stability: An emergency fund provides peace of mind, reducing financial stress and anxiety.
3. To Bare Or Avoid Debt: By having a cushion, you can avoid going into debt when unexpected expenses arise.

How Much Should You Save

- Aim For 3-6 Months' Worth Of Expenses: This amount can help you cover unexpected expenses, such as: - Car repairs: $500-$1,000,   - Medical bills: $1,000-$2,000,   - Apartment damages: $500-$1,000.
- Consider Your Circumstances: If you have a part-time job or irregular income, you may want to save more.

Where To Keep Your Emergency Fund

- High-Yield Savings Account: Earn interest on your savings while keeping your money easily accessible.
- Money Market Fund: A low-risk investment option that provides liquidity.

Tips For Building Your Emergency Fund

- Start Small: Set aside a manageable amount each month, even if it's just $20.
- Automate Your Savings: Set up automatic transfers from your checking account.
- Review And Adjust: Regularly review your emergency fund and adjust as needed.

Common Mistakes To Avoid

- Not Having An Emergency Fund: Don't assume you'll always have time to react to unexpected expenses.
- Using Your Emergency Fund For Non-essentials: Keep your emergency fund separate from your everyday spending money.

By following these guidelines, you'll be better equipped to handle unexpected expenses and maintain financial stability throughout your student journey. Remember, an emergency fund is a crucial component of a comprehensive student budget plan.

PART 3: PRACTICAL TIPS AND STRATEGIES

Chapter 10: Saving Money On A Student Budget

Finding Student Discounts

Many businesses offer discounts to students. Take advantage of:

- Student ID Benefits: Always carry your student ID to access discounts on public transportation, software, and local businesses.
- Online Deals: Use websites and apps that aggregate student discounts.

Saving On Textbook And Supplies

Textbooks can be a significant expense. You can save money by:

- Buying Used: Purchase second-hand books from online marketplaces or campus stores.
- Renting: Rent textbooks for the semester.
- Digital Versions: Opt for e-books or digital resources at times.

Affordable Meal Planning

As a student, eating well doesn't have to break the bank. With a little planning, you can enjoy delicious and nutritious meals while staying within your budget.

Benefits Of Meal Planning

- Saves Money: Plan meals around sales and affordable ingredients.
- Reduces Food Wastage: Use up leftovers and avoid buying too much food.

- Eats Healthier: Plan balanced meals and avoid relying on fast food or takeout.
- Saves Time: Cook meals in bulk and have leftovers for busy days.

Tips For Affordable Meal Planning

- Plan Meals Around Staples: Focus on affordable ingredients like rice, beans, and pasta.
- Shop Sales: Check weekly ads and plan meals around discounted items.
- Buy In Bulk: Purchase non-perishable items in bulk to save money.
- Cook In Bulk: Prepare large batches of food and freeze for later.
- Use Leftovers: Get creative with leftover ingredients to reduce waste.
- Cook at Home: Cook more at home to save time and money.
- Grocery Sales: Shop during sales and use coupons.
- Meal Prep: Plan your meals for the week to avoid eating out.

Budget-Friendly Meal Ideas
- Pasta with marinara sauce and veggies:

- Black bean and rice bowls:

- Grilled cheese sandwiches and soup:

- Stir-fry with frozen veggies and rice:

- Omelets with veggies and toast:

Grocery Shopping On A Budget
1. Shop At Discount Stores: Consider Aldi or Lidl for affordable staples.
2. Use Cashback Apps: Apps like Ibotta and Fetch Rewards offer cashback on groceries.
3. Buy Generic Or Store-brand Products: Often cheaper than name-brand products.

By following these tips and meal ideas, you can enjoy affordable and delicious meals while staying within your budget. Remember, meal planning is a key component of a comprehensive student budget plan.

Chapter 11:
Frugal Living Tips

Cost Effective Housing Options

Housing is a major expense for students. Consider:
- Roommates: Share living costs by having roommates.
- Off-campus Housing: Sometimes renting off-campus can be cheaper than dorms.
- Campus Housing Resources: Utilize university resources for affordable housing options.

Entertainment On A Budget

Enjoy your schooling without blowing up finances:
- Free Events: Attend campus events that are free or low-cost.
- Student Activities: Join clubs and societies for low-cost socializing.
- Streaming Services: Share subscriptions with friends to save on entertainment costs.

Second-Hand Shopping

Money management can be difficult for students. Embracing secondhand shopping is an efficient approach to saving money. This sub-chapter will examine the advantages and strategies for incorporating second-hand shopping into your student lifestyle.

Benefits Of Second-Hand Shopping

1. Saves Money: Second-hand items are significantly cheaper than buying new ones.
2. Reduce Waste: Buying second-hand reduces the demand for new, resource-intensive products.
3. Unique Finds: Thrift stores and online marketplaces often carry one-of-a-kind items.
4. Sustainable Fashion: Second-hand shopping promotes sustainable fashion and reduces fast fashion's environmental impact.

Tips For Second-Hand Shopping

- Thrift Stores: Explore local charity shops, Goodwill, and Salvation Army stores.

- Online Marketplaces: Utilize platforms like eBay, Craigslist, Facebook Marketplace, and local online selling groups.
- Consignment Stores: Visit stores that sell gently used items, often at a higher quality than thrift stores.
- Garage Sales and Estate Sales: Keep an eye out for sales in your neighborhood or community.
- Inspect Before Buying: Always check the condition and quality of items before purchasing.
- Negotiate: Don't be afraid to negotiate prices, especially at garage sales or with online sellers.
- Shop During Sales: Take advantage of discounts and promotions at thrift stores and online marketplaces.

Second-Hand Shopping Essentials For Students

- Textbooks: Buy used textbooks or rent them for a semester.
- Furniture: Find affordable, gently used furniture for your dorm room or apartment.
- Clothing: Update your wardrobe with second-hand clothing and accessories.

- Electronics: Purchase refurbished or used electronics, like laptops or phones.
- Housewares: Find second-hand kitchenware, bedding, and other essentials for your living space.

By embracing second-hand shopping, you'll not only save money but also contribute to a more sustainable lifestyle. Happy thrifting!

Chapter 12:
Increasing Your Income

Part-Time Jobs And Gigs

Boost your income with:

- On-campus Jobs: Look for jobs offered by your university.
- Freelancing: Offer skills like tutoring, writing, or graphic design online.
- Gig Economy: Participate in gigs like food delivery or ridesharing.

Freelancing Opportunities

Learn, Or Capitalize on your skills:

- Freelance Websites: Join platforms like Upwork, Fiverr, Freelancer, and others for online part time jobs.
- Build a Portfolio: Showcase your work to attract clients.
- Network: Connect with potential clients through social media and professional networks.

Scholarships And Grants

Exploring scholarships and grants is an excellent approach to financing your education. These types of financial aid can significantly enhance your budget, allowing you to meet tuition, living expenses, and other educational costs.

What Are Scholarships

Scholarships are merit-based or need-based awards that can be used to fund your education. They're usually offered by universities, colleges, organizations, or individuals. Scholarships can be competitive, so it's essential to research and apply to multiple opportunities.

Types Of Scholarships

- Merit-based Scholarships: Awarded to students with exceptional academic achievements, talents, or skills.
- Need-based Scholarships: Provided to students who demonstrate financial need.
- Field-specific Scholarships: Offered to students pursuing a specific field of study, like STEM or arts.
- Diversity Scholarships: Awarded to students from underrepresented groups, promoting diversity and inclusion.

What Are Grants

Grants are need-based awards that provide funding for students who demonstrate financial need. Unlike loans, grants don't require repayment. Grants can be federal, state, or institutional, and are often awarded based on the FAFSA (Free Application for Federal Student Aid).

Types Of Grants

1. Federal Pell Grant: A need-based grant for undergraduate students.
2. Federal Supplemental Educational Opportunity Grant (FSEOG): A need-based grant for undergraduate students.
3. State Grants: Offered by state governments to residents pursuing higher education.
4. Institutional Grants: Provided by colleges and universities to their students.

Tips For Applying

- Research Thoroughly: Explore various scholarship and grant opportunities.
- Meet Deadlines: Submit applications well before the deadlines.
- Tailor Your Applications: Customize your essays and materials for each opportunity.

- Follow Up: Confirm receipt of your application and materials.
- Combine Awards: Stack scholarships and grants to maximize your funding.

Additional Resources

1. Fastweb: A comprehensive scholarship search platform.
2. (link unavailable): A popular scholarship search engine.
3. College Board: A website offering scholarship, and grant resources.
4. FAFSA: Complete the Free Application for Federal Student Aid to determine your eligibility for grants and other financial aid.

Other top scholarship search engines and websites: Scholarships.com, CareerOneStop, Chegg, Cappex, Scholarships, College Board's Scholarship Search, Peterson's, Niche, Unigo, Sallie Mae, Scholly, Scholarship Owl.

By exploring scholarships and grants, you can unlock free money to fund your education and achieve your academic goals. Remember to stay organized, persistent, and creative in your search for financial aid. Good luck!

Chapter 13:
Investment Basics For Students

Introduction To Investing

Investing can help grow your money over time. The best way to start is by understanding the 3 investment basics for students :

1. Understand Risk and Reward: All investments involve some level of risk. Generally, bigger potential profits are associated with higher risks. Determine your risk tolerance and invest accordingly. It is critical to understand the risk associated with each type of investment and fit it with your financial objectives and schedule.
2. Start Small and Stay Consistent: Begin with a modest amount of money, even if it's just a few dollars. Many investment platforms allow you to start with small amounts. Consistent, regular contributions can grow significantly over time due to compound interest.
3. Diversify Your Portfolio: Don't put all your money into a single investment. Spread your investments across different asset classes like stocks, bonds, and mutual funds to minimize risk. Diversification helps protect your investment from market volatility.

Why Invest

1. Wealth Creation: Investing helps your money grow faster than inflation.
2. Financial Independence: Build wealth for long-term goals, like retirement.

Investment Options

1. Stocks: Own a portion of companies, like Apple or Amazon.
2. Bonds: Lend money to governments or companies, earning interest.
3. Mutual Funds: Diversified portfolios managed by professionals.
4. Exchange-Traded Funds (ETFs): Similar to mutual funds but trade on stock exchanges.

Investing Strategies

- Tax-efficient Investing: Consider tax implications and optimize investments accordingly.
- Regular Portfolio Rebalancing: Periodically review and adjust investments to maintain desired asset allocation.

- Long-term Approach: Focus on long-term growth, rather than short-term gains.
- Dollar-cost Averaging: Invest a fixed amount regularly, regardless of market conditions.

- Diversification: Spread investments across asset classes, sectors, and geographies.
- Low-cost Investing: Minimize fees and expenses through index funds or ETFs.

- Value Investing: Look for undervalued stocks or assets with potential for growth.
- Growth Investing: Focus on companies or assets with high growth potential.

- Dividend Investing: Invest in dividend-paying stocks for regular income.
- Index Investing: Track a specific market index, like the S&P 500.

Remember, investing strategies should align with individual financial goals, risk tolerance, and time horizon. It's essential to educate yourself and consider consulting a financial advisor.

Getting Started
1. Open A Brokerage Account: Choose a reputable online broker.
2. Start Small: Invest a manageable amount regularly.
3. Educate yourself: Continuously learn about investing.
4. Seek Advice: Consult a financial advisor if needed.

Risk Management
1. Understand Risk Tolerance: Balance risk and potential returns.
2. Diversify: Spread investments to minimize risk.
3. Regularly Review: Adjust your portfolio as needed.

Micro Investing Apps And Resources
- Robinhood
- Acorns
- Stash
- Investopedia

Investing is a long-term game. Start early, be consistent, be patient, and you will be well on your way to building wealth.

Chapter 14: Planning For The Future

Building Credits

Good credit is essential for future financial needs. Build credit by:

- Using Credit Responsibly: Pay off your balance in full each month.
- Timely Payments: Never miss a payment to avoid late fees and damage to your credit score.
- Monitoring Credit: Regularly check your credit report for errors.

Understanding Insurance

Insurance protects against financial loss. Types to consider:

- Health Insurance: Essential for medical expenses.
- Renters Insurance: Protects personal possessions in the event of damage or loss.
- Auto Insurance: Required if you own a car.

Saving For Major Life Events

As a student, it's essential to consider long-term financial goals and save for significant life events, such as:

- Graduation and career launch
- Moving to a new city or country
- Getting married or entering a long-term partnership
- Buying a first home
- Starting a family
- Retirement
- Pursuing further education or certifications
- Major purchases (e.g., a car or investment property)
- Travel or sabbaticals
- Unexpected expenses or emergencies

Create A Long-term Savings Plan

- Identify your goals and priorities
- Set specific, achievable targets

- Determine the required savings amount and timeline
- Choose appropriate savings vehicles (e.g., high-yield accounts, investments, or retirement funds)
- Automate your savings through regular transfers
- Monitor and adjust your progress regularly

Strategies For Long-term Savings

1. Compound Interest: Leverage interest-earning accounts or investments.
2. Dollar-Cost Averaging: Consider investing a fixed amount consistently, irrespective of market conditions.
3. Tax-Advantaged Accounts: Utilize tax-deferred or tax-free accounts, such as 401(k), IRA, or Roth IRA.
4. Diversification: Spread savings across different asset classes, like stocks, bonds, or real estate.
5. Avoid lifestyle Inflation: Direct excess funds towards savings and investments.

Additional Tips
1. Prioritize needs over wants
2. Educate yourself on personal finance and investing
3. Avoid debt and high-interest loans
4. Build multiple income streams
5. Review and adjust your plan regularly

By saving for major life events, you'll be better prepared to achieve your long-term goals and secure your financial future. Remember to stay disciplined, patient, and informed about your savings journey.

PART 4: UTILIZING RESOURCES AND TOOLS

Chapter 15: Budgetting Tools And Apps

In today's digital age, managing your finances has never been easier thanks to the plethora of budgeting tools and apps available. These tools can simplify the process of tracking your expenses, setting financial goals, and ensuring you stay within your budget. This chapter will guide you through some of the most popular budgeting tools and apps that are particularly useful for students.

Mint

Overview

Mint is a comprehensive personal finance app that helps you manage your money, create budgets, and track spending. It connects to your bank accounts, credit cards, and other financial institutions to give you a real-time overview of your finances.

Features

- Budget Tracking: Automatically categorizes transactions and tracks spending against your set budget.
- Bill Reminders: Sends reminders for upcoming bills to avoid late fees.
- Financial Goals: Allows you to set and track financial goals, such as saving for a trip or paying off student loans.
- Credit Score Monitoring: Provides free credit score monitoring and tips to improve your score.

Pros

- User-friendly interface
- Comprehensive overview of your finances
- Free to use

Cons

- Ads can be intrusive
- Some features require linking to external accounts, which might raise security concerns

YNAB (You Need A Budget)

Overview

YNAB is designed to help users gain control over their money by following a set of rules that encourage mindful spending and saving. It's particularly popular among those who want a proactive approach to budgeting.

Features

- Four Rules System: Helps you allocate every dollar, plan for future expenses, and adjust your budget as needed.
- Goal Setting: Enables you to establish and track financial objectives.
- Real-Time Syncing: Syncs across multiple devices for real-time budget updates.
- Workshops and Support: Offers educational resources and live workshops to help you improve your budgeting skills.

Pros

- Encourages proactive financial planning
- Strong focus on educational resources
- Excellent customer support

Cons
- Monthly or annual subscription fee
- Requires a more hands-on approach compared to other apps

Pocket Guide

Overview

PocketGuard optimizes budgeting by displaying your disposable income after deducting expenses, goals, and essentials. It's designed for users who want a straightforward way to manage their finances without getting bogged down in details.

Features
- My Pocket: Displays the amount of money available for discretionary spending.
- Bill Tracking: Tracks upcoming bills and subscriptions.
- Spending Limits: Allows you to set limits on different spending categories.
- Savings Goals: Helps you set and track savings goals.

Pros

- Simple, easy-to-use interface
- Visual representation of disposable income
- Free version available

Cons

- Limited customization options
- Fewer features compared to more comprehensive apps

GoodBudget

Overview

Goodbudget uses the envelope budgeting method, which helps you allocate money to different spending categories, or "envelopes," ensuring you don't overspend in any area.

Festures

- Envelope Budgeting: Digital version of the traditional envelope method.
- Sync and Share: Syncs across devices and allows sharing budgets with family or roommates.
- Reports: Provides detailed reports on your spending habits.

Pros
- Simple and effective envelope system
- Ideal for collaborative budgeting
- Free and paid versions available

Cons
- May require more manual input compared to other apps
- Limited features in the free version

Wally

Overview

Wally is a personal finance app that focuses on expense tracking and budgeting, providing insights into your spending habits and helping you set financial goals.

Features
- Expense Tracking: Tracks expenses and categorizes them automatically.
- Budget Creation: Allows you to create and manage multiple budgets.

- Currency Support: Supports multiple currencies, making it ideal for international students.
- Financial Insights: Provides insights into your spending patterns

Pros
- Comprehensive expense tracking
- Supports multiple currencies
- Free to use

Cons
- New users may find the interface difficult.
- Limited customer support

Choosing The Right Tool For You

Selecting the right budgeting tool or app depends on your personal preferences and financial goals. Here are some factors to consider:

- Ease of Use: Choose an app that matches your comfort level with technology and financial management.

- Features: Ensure the app offers the features you need, such as bill tracking, goal setting, and spending analysis.

- Cost: Consider whether you're willing to pay for advanced features or if a free app meets your needs.

- Security: Verify the app's security measures, especially if you'll be linking your financial accounts

Budgeting tools and apps can be invaluable in helping you manage your finances effectively as a student. By leveraging the features and functionalities of these tools, you can gain better control over your money, make informed financial decisions, and work towards achieving your financial goals. Explore the options discussed in this chapter and choose the one that best fits your needs to start your journey toward financial stability and success

PART 5: STAYING MOTIVATED AND OVERCOMING CHALLENGES

Chapter 16: Staying On Track

Building Good Financial Habits

Creating and maintaining good financial habits is essential for long-term success. Here are some strategies:

- Consistent Tracking: Regularly update your budget and track your spending. This keeps you aware of where your money is going and helps you stay within your limits.

- Automatic Savings: Set up automatic transfers to your savings account. This ensures that you save a portion of your income regularly without having to think about it.

- Monthly Reviews: Schedule a monthly review of your budget to assess your progress, make necessary adjustments, and celebrate your successes.

Accountability Partners And Groups

Having someone to share your financial journey with can provide motivation and support:

- Find a Budget Buddy: Partner with a friend or family member who also wants to manage their finances. Share your goals and progress, and keep each other accountable.

- Join Financial Groups: Participate in local or online groups focused on financial literacy and budgeting. These groups can provide recommendations, motivation, and an overall sense of connection.

Self Reward

Sticking to a budget as a scholar can be challenging. It's essential to acknowledge and reward yourself for your hard work and financial discipline. Rewarding yourself can help you:

- Stay motivated: Celebrate milestones to maintain enthusiasm for budgeting.
- Reduce stress: Treat yourself to relaxation and enjoyment.
- Improve mental health: Recognize achievements and boost self-esteem.
- Create a balance: Enjoy life while maintaining financial responsibility.

By incorporating rewards into your budget, you'll create a more sustainable and enjoyable financial journey. Keep pushing forward, and remember to celebrate your successes along the way!

Rewarding Yourself Smartly

Rewarding yourself for sticking to your budget is essential, but it's equally important to do so smartly. Here's how:

- Don't Overdo It: Rewards should be occasional and within your budget.
- Stay Mindful: Avoid overspending or sabotaging your financial progress.
- Celebrate Milestones: Acknowledge your achievements and reflect on your journey.

- Choose Rewards That Align With Your Values: Select rewards that bring you joy and align with your financial goals.
- Make It Affordable: Ensure rewards fit within your budget and don't compromise your financial progress.
- Prioritize experiences over material goods: Invest in memories, like trying a new restaurant or attending a concert, rather than buying stuff.

- Use the 50/30/20 rule: Allocate 50% of your reward towards savings, 30% towards discretionary spending, and 20% towards debt repayment or investments.

- Avoid impulse purchases: Plan your rewards in advance to avoid making impulsive financial decisions.

- Consider free or low-cost alternatives: Find free or low-cost ways to reward yourself, like trying a new recipe or going for a hike.

- Review and adjust: Regularly assess your reward system to ensure it aligns with your financial goals and values.

- Set small goals and rewards: Achieve specific financial milestones, like saving a certain amount of money, or completing a budgeting challenge.

- Make it personal: Reward yourself with something meaningful, like a favorite meal or activity.
- Schedule rewards: Plan and look forward to your rewards.

Ideas For Rewards

1. Fun Activities: You can try a new restaurant, watch a movie, a play, a sporting event, or attend a concert.
2. Relaxation And Wellness: You can get a massage, take a bath or spa, take a yoga class, or practice meditation.
3. Hobbies And Interests: You can pursue a passion project, buy art supplies, a book, an online course, or learn a new skill.
4. Savings Boost: You can allocate a portion of your reward to your savings or emergency fund
5. A weekend getaway or staycation
6. A potluck or game night with friends

By rewarding yourself smartly, you'll maintain motivation, enjoy your hard-earned money, and stay on track with your financial goals. Remember, budgeting is about balance, not deprivation

Chapter 17:
Overcoming Common Challenges

Dealing With Peer Pressure

Peer pressure can cause overspending and financial difficulty. Here are few tips to help you cope with them.

- Communicate Your Goals: Let your friends know about your financial goals and budget constraints.

- Genuine friends will respect and support your decisions.

- Suggest Affordable Activities: Propose cost-effective alternatives when making plans with friends, like a potluck dinner instead of dining out.

- Stick to Your Budget: Firmly adhere to your budget. Remember that your financial health is more important than keeping up with others.

Coping With Financial Stress

Financial stress can be overwhelming, especially for students managing academic responsibilities. These few tips can help you cope:

- Acknowledge And Accept: Recognize your financial stress and accept it as a common challenge.
- Identify Triggers: Pinpoint specific financial stressors, such as tuition or living expenses.
- Prioritize Self-Care: Make time for activities promoting mental well-being, like exercise, meditation, or hobbies.
- Seek Support: Talk to friends, family, or a counselor about your financial concerns.
- Stay Organized: Keep track of finances, deadlines, and responsibilities using a planner or app.
- Focus On What You Can Control: Concentrate on managing your expenses and staying within your budget.
- Practice Gratitude: Reflect on the things you're thankful for, no matter how small.

- Take Breaks: Allow yourself time to relax and recharge.
- Seek Financial Assistance: Explore available resources, such as financial aid, scholarships, or emergency loans.
- Stay Positive: Remind yourself that financial stress is temporary and manageable.

Additionally, consider these strategies:
- Financial Journaling: Record your thoughts and feelings about money to process and release emotions.
- Budgeting Workshops: Attend seminars or online courses to improve financial literacy and skills.
- Campus Resources: Utilize counseling services, financial advisors, or student support groups.
- Mindful Spending: Practice mindful consumption and prioritize needs over wants.

Remember, coping with financial stress is a process. Be patient, kind, and compassionate with yourself as you work towards achieving financial stability and peace of mind.

Strategies For Staying Motivated

Staying motivated to budget can be a bit challenging, but these strategies can help you remain afloat.

- Visualize Your Goals: Create visual reminders of your financial goals, like a vision board or a chart tracking your progress.

- Stay Educated: Continuously educate yourself about personal finance through books, articles, podcasts, and workshops. Knowledge can be empowering and motivating.

- Reflect on Your Achievements: Regularly reflect on how far you've come. Recognize the positive changes in your financial habits and celebrate your successes

More Tips For Self-Motivation

Creating and sticking to a budget as a scholar can be challenging. Staying motivated is crucial to achieving your financial goals. So therefore, in other to stay motivated here are a few tips that can help:

- Set Clear Financial goals: Define what you want to achieve, whether it's saving for tuition or building an emergency fund.
- Track Your Progress: Regularly monitor your spending and savings to see how far you've come.
- Celebrate Milestones: Reward yourself for reaching budgeting milestones, like completing a month without overspending.
- Find Accountability: Share your budget with a trusted friend or family member and ask them to hold you accountable.
- Stay Positive: Focus on the benefits of budgeting, such as reduced stress and increased financial freedom.
- Make It A Habit: Incorporate budgeting into your daily routine, like checking your accounts or planning meals.
- Seek Inspiration: Follow personal finance bloggers, podcasts, or social media accounts for motivation and tips.

- Be Kind To Yourself: Don't be too hard on yourself if you slip up – simply get back on track.
- Visualize Your Future: Remember why you're budgeting and how it will improve your life in the long run.
- Stay Flexible: Adjust your budget as needed to stay motivated and on track.

Additionally, consider implementing the following:

- Budgeting Challenges: Try a "no-spend" month or a savings challenge to stay engaged.
- Budgeting Apps: Utilize apps like Mint, You Need a Budget (YNAB), or Personal Capital to track your finances and stay motivated.
- Financial Vision Board: Create a visual representation of your financial goals to stay focused.

By following these tips, you'll stay motivated and committed to your budget, achieving financial stability and success. Remember, budgeting is a journey, and every small step counts!

PART 6: REFLECTION

Chapter 18: Reflecting On Your Financial Journey

Measuring Your Progress

Tracking your progress is crucial to maintaining motivation and ensuring you stay on the right path:

- Regular Check-ins: Schedule regular intervals (monthly, quarterly) to review your budget and financial goals.

- Adjust as Needed: Be flexible and willing to adjust your budget and goals based on your progress and any changes in your financial situation.

Celebrating Your Achievements

Acknowledge and celebrate your financial milestones

- Small Wins: Recognize small achievements, like sticking to your budget for a month or saving a set amount.
- Major Milestones: Celebrate significant accomplishments, such as paying off a loan or reaching a savings goal.

Continuing Your Financially Education

Personal finance is a lifelong journey. Continue to educate yourself and improve your financial literacy:

- Stay Informed: Keep up with financial news and trends.
- Learn Continuously: Take advantage of educational resources like books, online courses, and seminars.
- Seek Advice: Don't hesitate to consult financial experts when needed.

By staying motivated and overcoming challenges, you'll build a solid foundation for a healthy financial future. Remember, budgeting is not just about limiting spending; it's about making informed decisions and achieving your financial goals. Keep moving forward, stay committed, and enjoy the journey to financial well-being.

GLOSSARY: Financial Terms

- Assets: Things you own that have value, such as money, investments, or property.

- Budget: A plan for how you will spend your money.

- Compound Interest: Interest earned on both the principal amount and any accrued interest.

- Credit Score: A number that shows how well you manage credit.

- Debt: Money you owe to someone else.

- Emergency Fund: Savings set aside for unexpected expenses.

- Expenses: Costs you incur to live, learn, and enjoy life.

- Financial Aid: Assistance to help pay for education expenses.

- Fixed Expenses: Regular costs that stay the same, like rent or phone bills.

- Interest Rate: The percentage of your loan or credit card balance charged as interest.

    (continued on next page)

- Investment: Putting money into something that may grow in value.

- Liability: Debts or financial obligations.

- Net Worth: The total value of your assets minus liabilities.

- Needs vs. Wants: Essential expenses (needs) vs. discretionary spending (wants).

- Savings: Money set aside for future use.

- Variable Expenses: Costs that change, like food or entertainment.

- APR (Annual Percentage Rate): The total cost of borrowing, including fees.

- FICO Score: A type of credit score used to evaluate creditworthiness.

- IRA (Individual Retirement Account): A savings account for retirement.

- Roth IRA: A type of IRA with tax-free growth and withdrawals.

Note: This glossary is not exhaustive, but it covers key terms relevant to student budgeting.

CONCLUSION

"In conclusion, Student Budget Guide has explored the complexities of budgeting and provided a comprehensive guide for students. Through the 18 chapters, we have delved into the key concepts, strategies, and best practices for financial independence.

Our journey has taken us from the fundamentals to advanced techniques, equipping you with the knowledge and tools to reach your financial goals. As you close this book after your first read, remember that this is not where the journey ends, this is where it begins.

This book is a companion that you can always come back to. Read it as many times as you can, and apply the insights and wisdom gained from these pages to push you up to that financial level that you desire to get. Thank you for joining me on this journey, and I wish you continued success and growth all through your academic journey ."

www.ingramcontent.com/pod-product-compliance
Lightning Source LLC
Chambersburg PA
CBHW070354230526
45471CB00006B/2558